A Hut of One's Own

A Hut of One's Own

How to Make the Most of Your Allotment Shed

Reclaimed bricks

Illustrated by Emily Chappell

HEAD OF ZEUS

Printed and bound in Italy
by L.E.G.O. S.p.A.

Head of Zeus Ltd
First Floor East
5–8 Hardwick Street
London EC1R 4RG

www.headofzeus.com

For John Richard Chappell

Contents

Introduction   01

Allotment Entrances   02
A Shed of One's Own   04
Greenhouses of Note   14
Little Ones   20
Making a Statement   22
A Shed Made a Home   28
Park Your Bum   34
Sanctuary for All   38
Signs   42
Earth...   44
...Wind...   48
...and Fire   50
Stoves   52
The Great Downpour   54

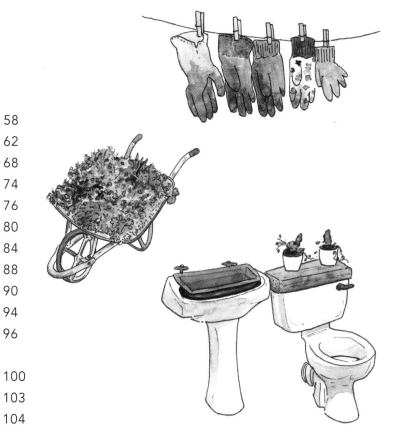

Borders	58
Planters	62
Nurture	68
Weed Control	74
Protection	76
Rogues Gallery	80
Storage	84
Harnessing the Sun	88
Communal Huts	90
En Suite Bathrooms	94
Ornamental Flourishes	96
Useful Information	100
With Thanks	103
About the Author	104

Introduction

I have a confession to make. I am a magpie, a scavenger, a cheapskate. Whatever you want to call it, I love skip diving, salvaging and getting stuff for free. I like to claim other people's junk and make something either useful or beautiful out of it. And I'm not alone.

It's some sort of unwritten code for allotment gardeners – you must get materials for free, and if not for free, then dirt cheap. People new to allotmenting soon adopt the code, as fellow growers love nothing more than sharing their recent acquisitions – windows from an old conservatory, thrown-out scaffolding netting, redundant patio furniture... I've seen shower-door cold frames, gas-bottle woodburning stoves, and huts made entirely out of stripped-down pallets. No piece of junk can be underestimated when it comes to building structures on an allotment site.

So here's to the self-build – the inventions, the recycling, the follies... Those flat-pack sheds? Forget it. I've seen too many crumple at the mere suggestion of a high wind! Let's champion the individual, their ingenuity, and the community spirit and on-site bartering that greases the wheel.

Allotment Entrances

Some allotments have open plans and no clear boundaries... others are separated by hedges, walls or fences... and some have their own stylised doors.

- Adapt wooden pallets to make both gates and fences... and pretty much any other useful structure on an allotment site.

- Build an arch out of plastic tubing and fix it above a gate to let climbing plants take over.

- Recycle old garden gates from home.

Cat entrance?

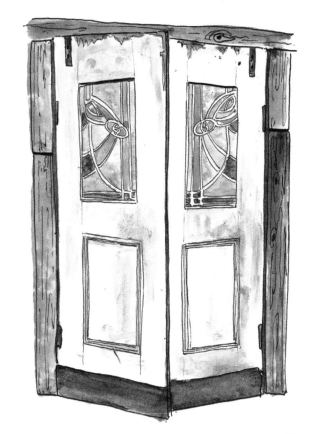

A Shed of One's Own

Not all allotment associations allow for the freedom of building your own shed, greenhouse or stove. If you are lucky enough to not have these restrictions, building and ongoing repairs are an enjoyable and integral part of allotment life. The shed, or hut, is often the heart of the plot – a place for storage, shelter, organisation and tea breaks. They are also expressions of our personalities, tastes and whims.

- All hail, the pallet! Don't underestimate the power of the pallet! You can pretty much build anything out of them, and they're in plentiful supply on most allotment sites.

- Old windows are perfect for making your own greenhouse or shed with a view.

- Set aside gleaned roofing felt, tough plastic, corrugated iron, etc. for roof repairs.

- If you've inherited a rickety shed, consider ways of repairing and adapting it first before starting again on your own structure. You'll learn how to both repair and construct, finding out what you consider essential along the way – size, storage, location, orientation, etc.

Plastic corrugated roofing

Roofing felt

Frosted glass door

Coat hooks

Corrugated roofing (aluminium)

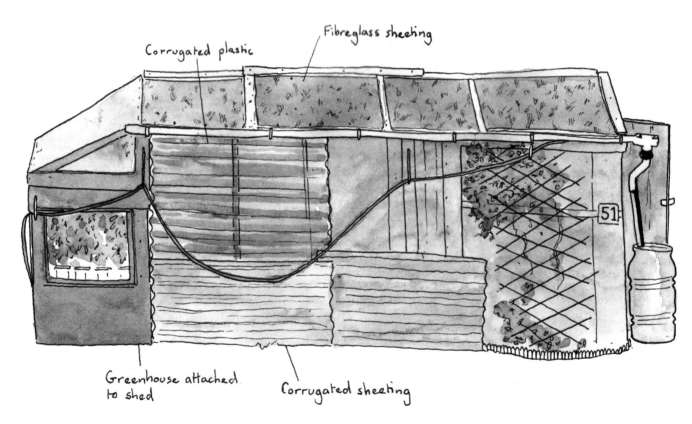

Corrugated plastic

Fibreglass sheeting

51

Greenhouse attached to shed

Corrugated sheeting

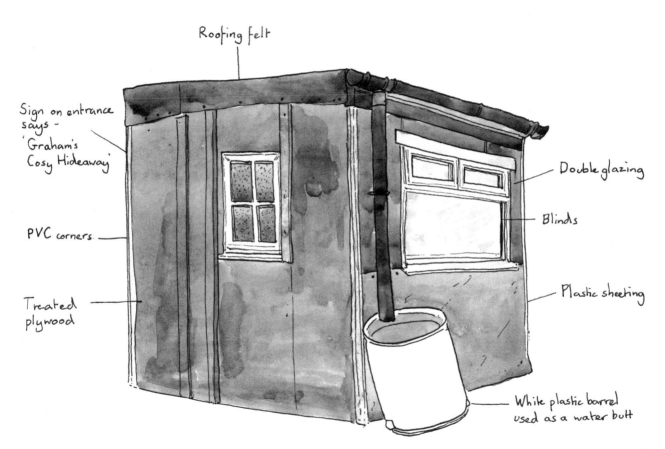

Roofing felt

Sign on entrance
says -
'Graham's
Cosy Hideaway'

Double glazing

Blinds

PVC corners.

Treated
plywood

Plastic sheeting

White plastic barrel
used as a water butt

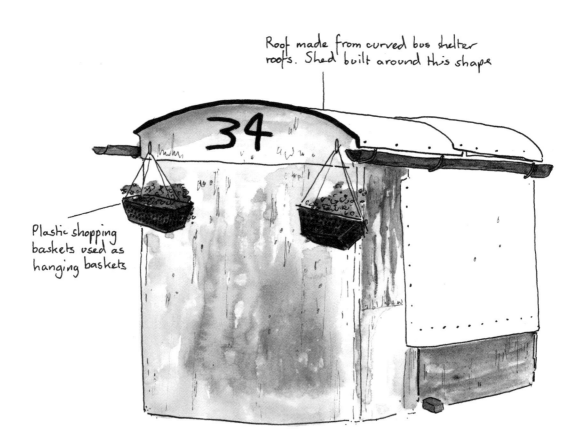

Roof made from curved bus shelter roofs. Shed built around this shape

Plastic shopping baskets used as hanging baskets

34

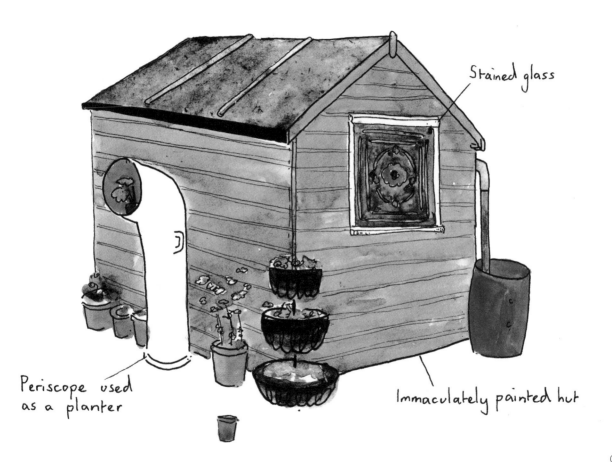

Stained glass

Periscope used as a planter

Immaculately painted hut

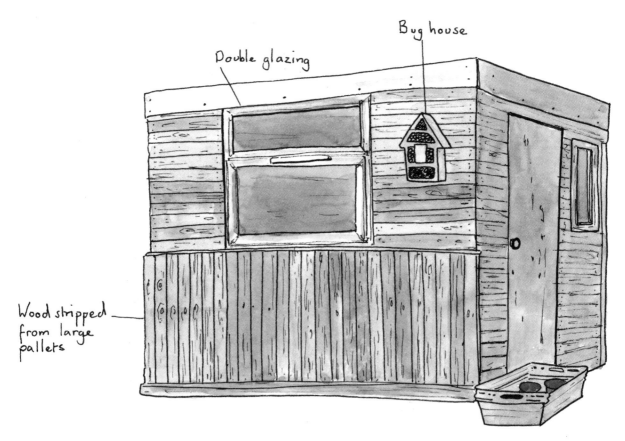

Double glazing

Bug house

Wood stripped from large pallets

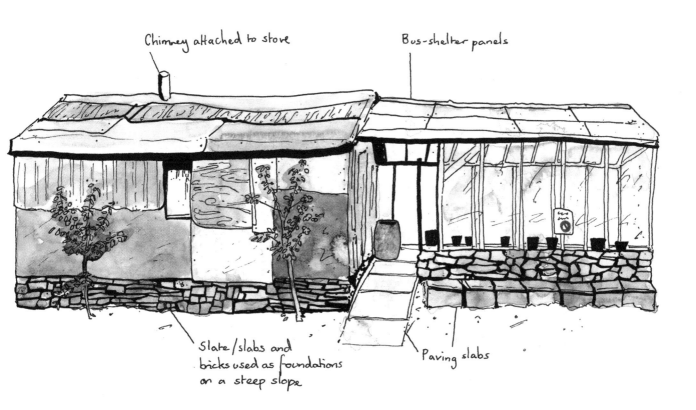

Chimney attached to store

Bus-shelter panels

Slate/slabs and bricks used as foundations on a steep slope

Paving slabs

All windows and doors are from old conservatories

Sacks for potatoes

Plastic sheeting from a famous clothes shop's window display

Aluminium sheeting covers the wooden structure - lithographic printing plates recycled from a local printing works

Patio furniture

Outhouse doors

13

Greenhouses of Note

Some greenhouses are attached to the hut or are built as one – the structure being a combination of the two. Other greenhouses are built separately and have a beauty of their own.

- Polytunnels are a common sight on allotments. You can make them by starting with a basic raised bed base, then adding a timber frame at the entrance. The arches can be made using tough tubing (like the blue pipes used for water mains), with corrugated plastic or UVI (Ultra Violet Inhibited) polythene to cover them.

- Greenhouse panes can be either glass or plastic. Glass is best, but it can be easily damaged and a target for vandals. Some gardeners cover their greenhouse roofs with plastic mesh to prevent damage.

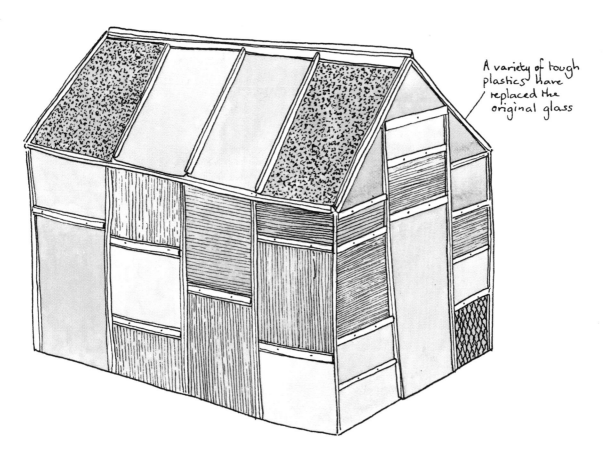

A variety of tough plastics have replaced the original glass

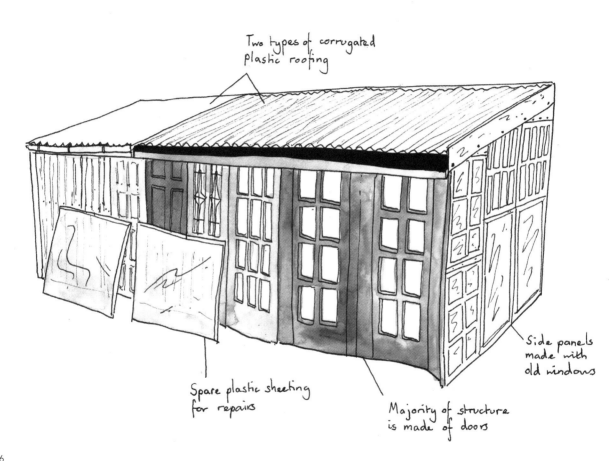

Two types of corrugated plastic roofing

Side panels made with old windows

Spare plastic sheeting for repairs

Majority of structure is made of doors

Greenhouse made from stacked plastic bottles, wire and reclaimed wood

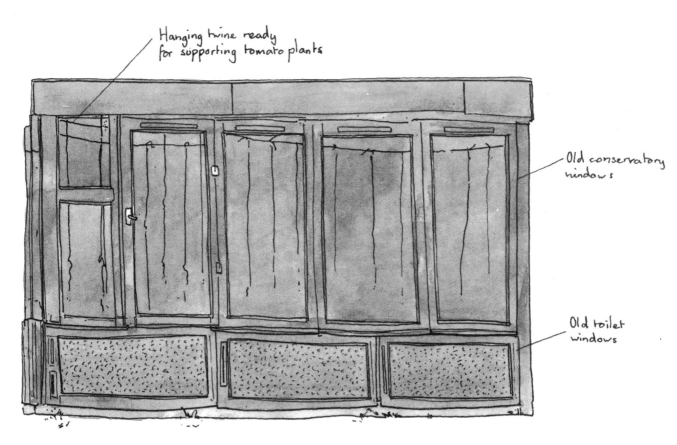

Hanging twine ready for supporting tomato plants

Old conservatory windows

Old toilet windows

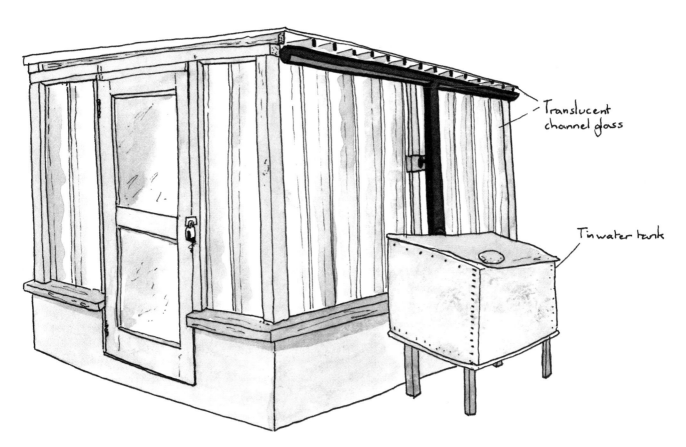

Translucent
channel glass

Tin water tank

19

Little Ones

Children are hard-wired to love the excitement of nature on an allotment – eating freshly picked peas, watching tadpoles turn into frogs, growing giant sunflowers and collecting worms... But you can't expect them to remain captivated for ever...

- Build a den or hideout together.

- Give them a small patch of land to look after themselves.

Entire hut made from recycled advertising panels (treated with wood preserver)

Plastic tubing -weatherproof

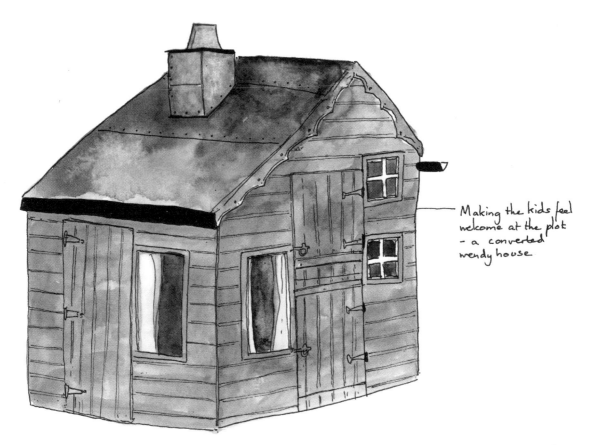

Making the kids feel welcome at the plot – a converted wendy house

Making a Statement

Sometimes a little bit of inspired thinking or a noble experiment can lead to some impressive architecture, or a visually playful building. And sometimes, when the integrity of an existing structure is maintained, and it remains intact on the allotment, the unique character of the original is imparted wholesale too. I'm thinking air-raid shelters, train carriages, old caravans...

- Make it surreal. Make it colourful. Make it larger than it needs to be (within the allotment association guidelines, of course).

- Listen to your inner child – yes, building a pirate ship-themed shed would be most appropriate.

- Research different architectural styles – Art Nouveau, Gothic, Postmodern, etc.

The shed as canvas

Pot ornament

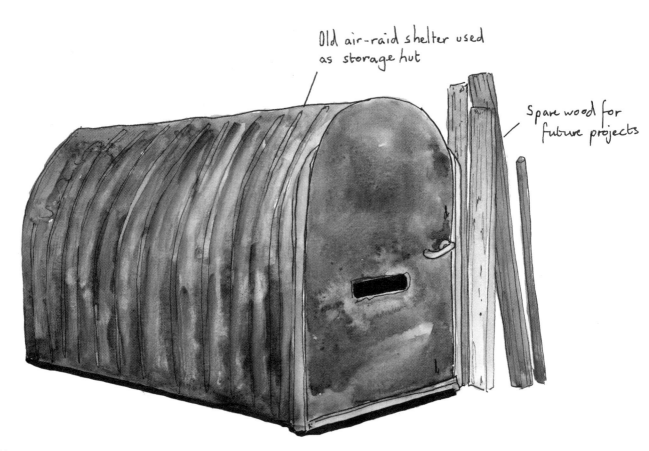

Old air-raid shelter used as storage hut

Spare wood for future projects

Mock-Tudor style

Herb garden

42

Old bus shelter panels used to make a hut. The plotholder has added his own graffiti on top of what was already there

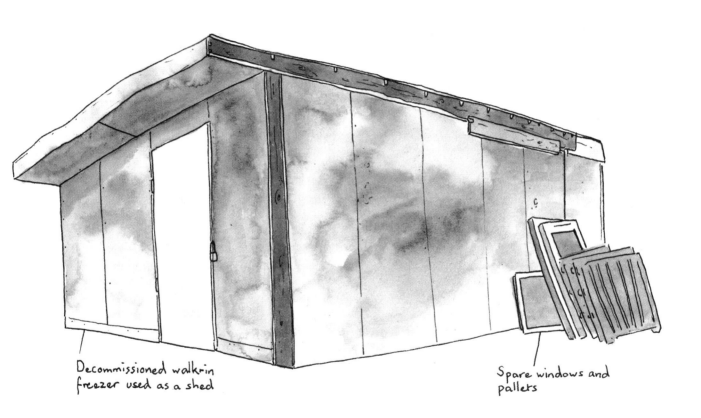

Decommissioned walk-in
freezer used as a shed

Spare windows and
pallets

A Shed Made a Home

Whether you like solitude or company, cosiness or controlled chaos, fitting out your shed to your taste will make allotment life run smoothly. Beyond the essentials of tool storage and protection from the elements, allotment sheds are places to meet, think, plan, eat and drink.

- Be on the lookout for old furniture – settees, chairs, bookshelves and coffee tables.

- Keep food and seeds in airtight containers (coffee canisters, biscuit tins, etc.), away from the reach of mice.

- Invest in a camping stove or attach a hotplate to your woodburning stove.

Gas camping
hob and grill

Courgette
frittata

Homemade
bread

SLUG KILLER

Old policemen's lockers

Log store - grower being a woodworker/ artist

Spare tile

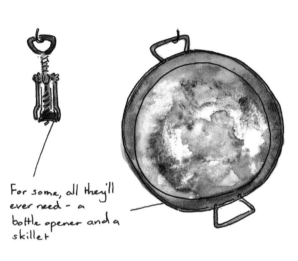

For some, all they'll ever need - a bottle opener and a skillet

Toilet roll holder

Tomato Onion

Concentrated Organic Garlic Spray To deter (greenfly) Please dilute

BUND A

SPORTS ORANGE
2 FOR 90p

Plotholder shares some organic pest deterrent

Drink holder built into inside of shed

Art and prints found in skips are put on display in sheds

Park Your Bum

Most gardeners rarely sit down – there's too much work to be done. Friends and family probably won't always share this enthusiasm, so keep a stock of chairs and stools for visitors when it's BBQ season.

- Adopt thrown-out plastic patio furniture – it'll last a long time.

- Build something more traditional, for example, from tree stumps or spare wood.

- Make a bench that doubles up as a tool store.

- Acquire a deck chair, director's chair or lounger.

'Antique' seat

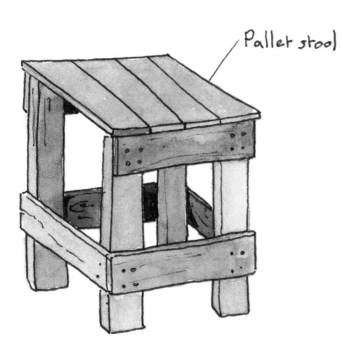

Pallet stool

Upcycled wooden stool

Football stadium
seating from local
club

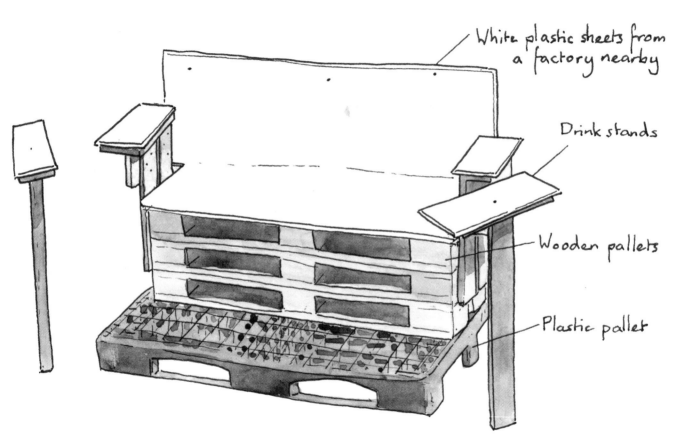

White plastic sheets from a factory nearby

Drink stands

Wooden pallets

Plastic pallet

Sanctuary For All

While some gardeners do their best to ward off birds, others encourage them to feel at home by providing bird feeders and nest boxes. Regardless of whether you appreciate wildlife or not, encouraging pollinators to stop by (insects, bees, moths), will mean that your crops and flowers flourish.

- There are many different types of bird box that you can build from scratch using bought or reclaimed wood. Make sure it's weather-proof, but not pressure-treated timber. Different birds like different-shaped boxes, and different-sized, and spaced entrance holes. Do your research!

- Keep a section of your plot undisturbed (no weeding needed!). Covered ground, branches and tree stumps will encourage wildlife to take refuge.

- Build a bug hotel using wooden pallets for the basic tiered structure. Examples of 'fillings' include hollow sticks or stems (like bamboo), ceramic pots, straw, hay, hessian, broken roof slates or roofing felt, pipes, straws, plastic bottles, bricks with holes in, pine cones...

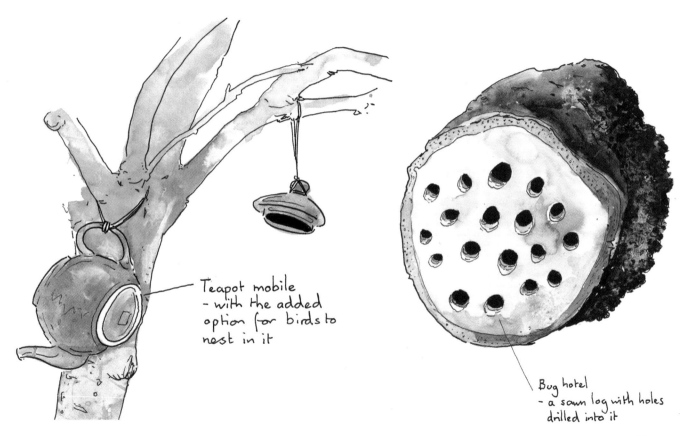

Teapot mobile
- with the added
option for birds to
nest in it

Bug hotel
- a sawn log with holes
drilled into it

Guttering

Roofing felt

Scaffolding board

Foundation built
from a pallet

Piece of decking

Roofing felt

Roof garden

41

Signs

Individual plots on an allotment site are numbered, so a sign will be required. Some gardeners add a further touch of flair with handcrafted signs and personalised plot names.

- Use driftwood, slate or spare pallet wood to make a plaque. Hang it up with wire, rope or spare string.

- Carve, spray-paint, stencil, print, mosaic…

Milk churn

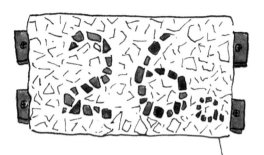

Broken ceramic tiles

Earth...

Soil is the most essential component of a functioning allotment. Unpolluted, nutrient-rich earth results in unpolluted, nutrient-rich vegetables. Most growers make their own compost and top up with locally sourced manure for more productivity. Some sites have shared composting facilities and/or bays to store manure deliveries, but most growers have composting systems on their own plots.

- Again, pallets (wooden or plastic) are the usual choice of material to build a compost bay. Use them as they are in their original state (tying corners together with cable ties or rope), or strip them down to create your own design with removable front panels.

- Avoid using pressure-treated wood – unknown chemicals could filter into your compost, and into your crops.

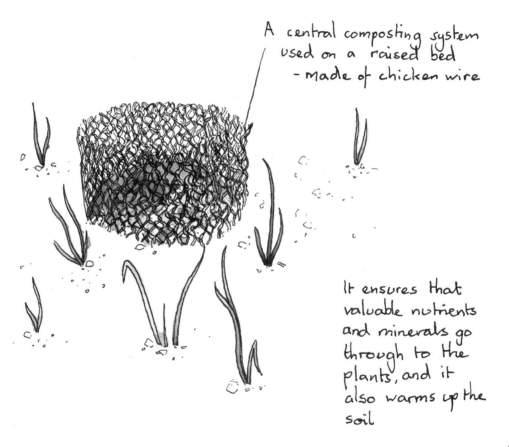

A central composting system used on a raised bed - made of chicken wire

It ensures that valuable nutrients and minerals go through to the plants, and it also warms up the soil

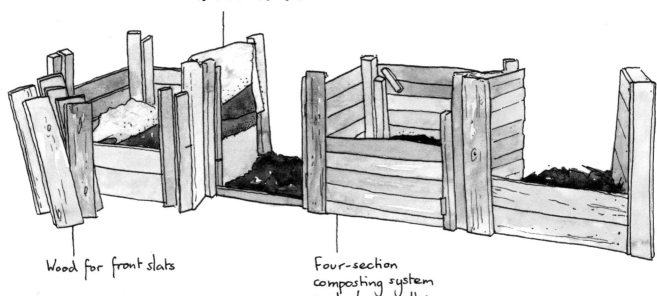

Old carpet placed on top of heaps to conserve heat

Wood for front slats

Four-section composting system made from pallet wood and other scrap wood

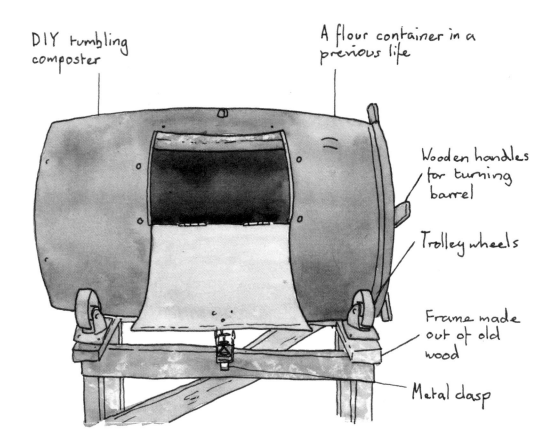

DIY tumbling composter

A flour container in a previous life

Wooden handles for turning barrel

Trolley wheels

Frame made out of old wood

Metal clasp

... Wind...

Strong winds put allotment structures to the test. In wild weather you can kiss goodbye to flimsy plastic polytunnels, greenhouses and poorly made 'flat pack' sheds.

- Polytunnels and other structures made with plastic film need weighing down so they don't blow away. Use rope and empty plastic milk containers filled with water to add ballast.

- When using sheet plastic, fix it tight so that the winds don't pick up and tear/damage the structure.

An old screwdriver keeping a greenhouse door shut in the absence of a padlock

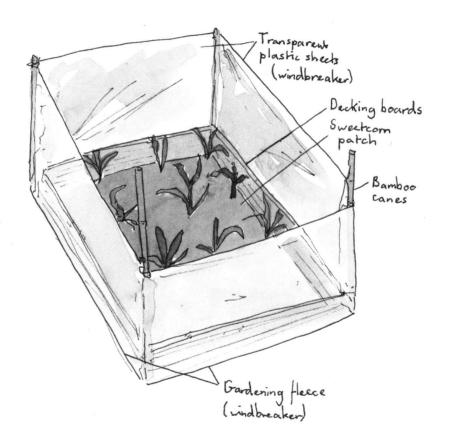

Transparent plastic sheets (windbreaker)

Decking boards

Sweetcorn patch

Bamboo canes

Gardening fleece (windbreaker)

... and Fire

Not all allotment sites allow you to burn waste, but if you can, it's a valuable investment to get hold of, or build, an incinerator.

- Old washing machine drums make great mini incinerators or BBQs.

- Place the burners on bricks to save burning the ground.

- Make sure not to burn treated wood or plastics.

Oil drum with holes drilled into it

Breezeblocks

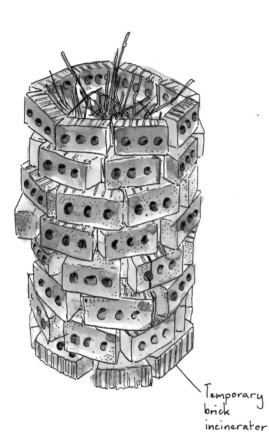

Temporary brick incinerator

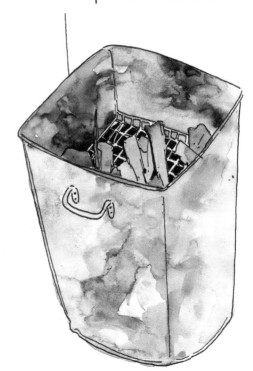

Metal lining of waste bin + mesh frame = incinerator

Stoves

Used for warmth and/or cooking, woodburning stoves are a reliable resource for all-season gardeners. You'll need a large enough shed and plenty of ventilation.

- All sorts of containers (that have been thoroughly washed out first) could be used as a stove cylinder – an oil drum, a large paint tin adapted to have a hinged lid/door, two steam trays joined together (bain-maries), a stainless-steel water pitcher...

- Place breezeblocks around the stove to keep in excess heat for the shed/greenhouse at night. This also prevents the heat from rising straight up and escaping...

- Make sure not to burn treated wood or plastics.

Exhaust pipe

Beer keg

Woodburner made from a propane bottle

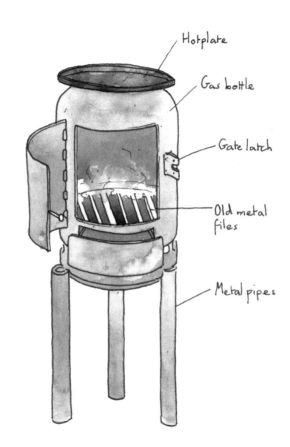

Hotplate

Gas bottle

Gate latch

Old metal files

Metal pipes

The Great Downpour

Rainwater is more beneficial for your plants than tap water, so it makes sense to harvest the rain. Guttering and water butts are the obvious choice for catching rain, with the option to syphon off water into other large containers for storage. There are advantages to living in a wet climate!

- Dustbins, steel drums, beer barrels and bulk catering containers can all be used as water butts. Make sure that nothing toxic has been kept in them though!

- IBC tanks (intermediate bulk containers) can be bought second-hand. These also make for good water storage.

- Use piping to syphon water into other water butts – the more storage, the better.

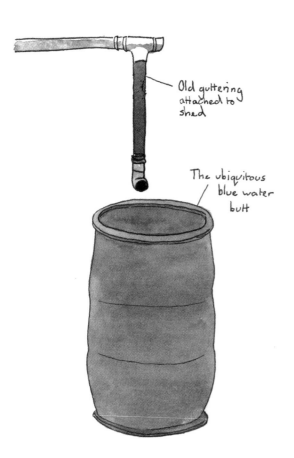

Old guttering attached to shed

The ubiquitous blue water butt

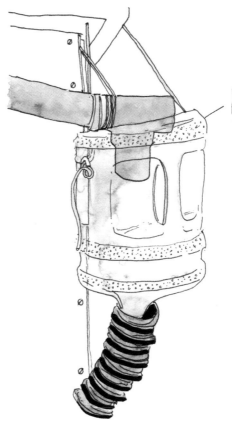

Water catcher for water butt - used what was available at the time (water bottle)

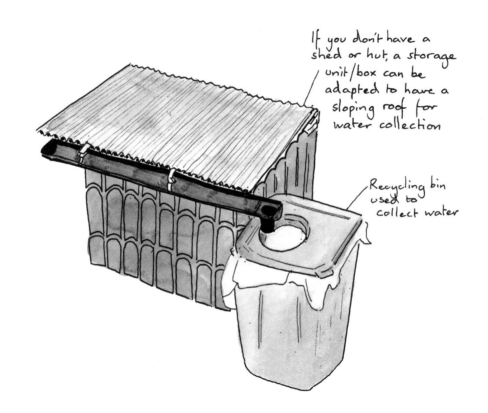

If you don't have a shed or hut, a storage unit/box can be adapted to have a sloping roof for water collection

Recycling bin used to collect water

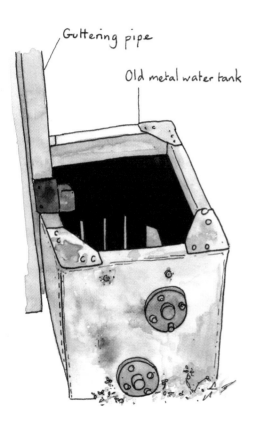

Guttering pipe

Old metal water tank

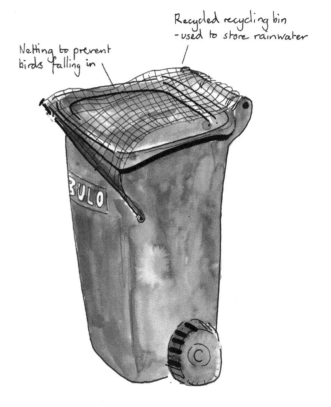

Netting to prevent birds falling in

Recycled recycling bin - used to store rainwater

BULO

Borders

Raised beds are an effective way of maximising space. They allow for tighter planting and are also a defence against ground frost. If the soil is potentially contaminated, they can also be used on top of plastic ground sheeting so that you have more control of the soil's make-up. Hedges or fencing are often necessary to mark out the boundaries of plots, and ornamental borders can be created within an individual plot for visual interest.

- Scaffolding planks are ideal for building raised beds.

- Large wooden pallets can be stripped down to build tall fencing.

- Cut pallet wood into short pieces to make an attractive raised bed border.

- Make a tessellated path out of salvaged bricks.

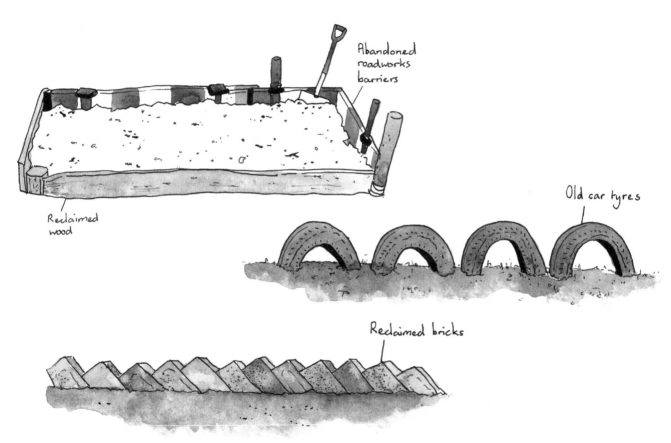

Abandoned roadworks barriers

Reclaimed wood

Old car tyres

Reclaimed bricks

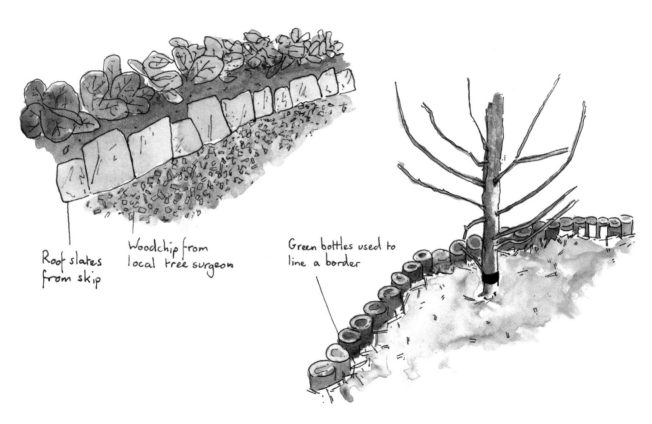

Roof slates
from skip

Woodchip from
local tree surgeon

Green bottles used to
line a border

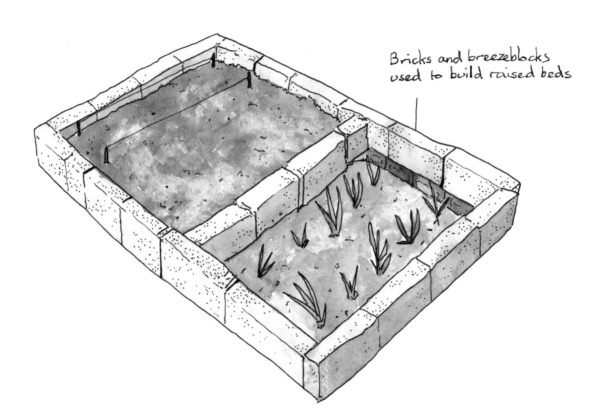

Bricks and breezeblocks used to build raised beds

Planters

Other than plastic and ceramic pots, all manner of containers can be used to house plants, bulbs and flowers.

- Tin cans and larger drums make interesting containers for bulbs.

- 1 tonne heavy-duty builders' bags are great for growing potatoes or other vegetables when space is at a premium.

- For a large-scale planter, reuse an old boat!

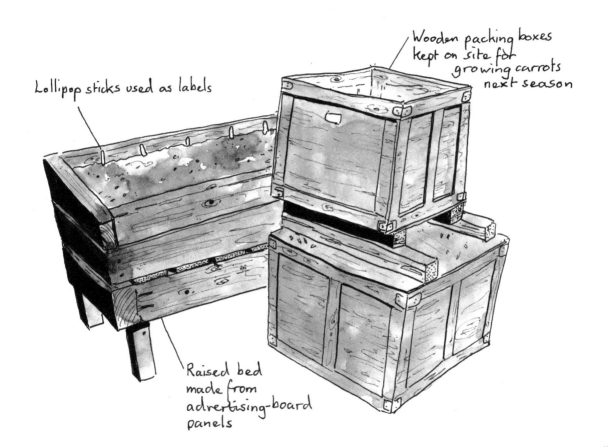

Lollipop sticks used as labels

Wooden packing boxes kept on site for growing carrots next season

Raised bed made from advertising-board panels

Vintage mobile
water container

Giant strawberry pots
made from plastic bins
with holes drilled into
them

Washing machine barrel used as a planter

An eccentric herb planter made from an abandoned piece of construction tubing

Painted car tyres used to make a tower to plant potatoes in - stack them higher as the plant grows

Holes to be drilled in the bottom for good drainage

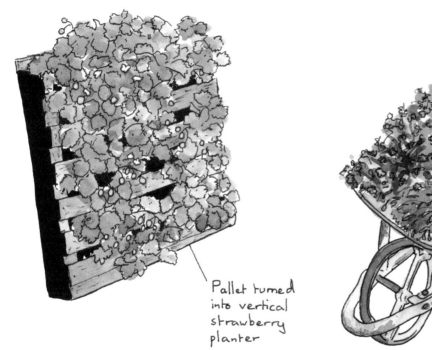

Pallet turned
into vertical
strawberry
planter

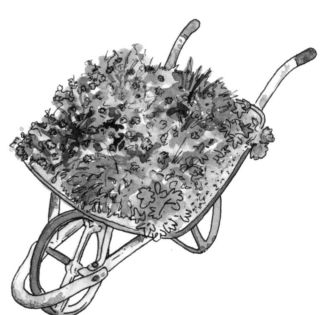

Nurture

After diligently sowing your seeds in a greenhouse, seedbed or cold frame, a little TLC is needed to encourage them as they continue to grow outside. Finding ways to raise the temperature just a few degrees can make all the difference to the plant's health.

- Cut plastic bottles in two and use each half as a mini greenhouse for individual plants. This is particularly effective in colder areas.

- Bubble wrap or fleecing can help protect plants in cold conditions. Polystyrene pots and trays are also helpful for insulation.

- Blanch celery by tying cardboard around the stalks – celery straitjackets!

Giant pot cloche
made from a
plastic water
bottle

Cold frame made
from an old
window and its
frame

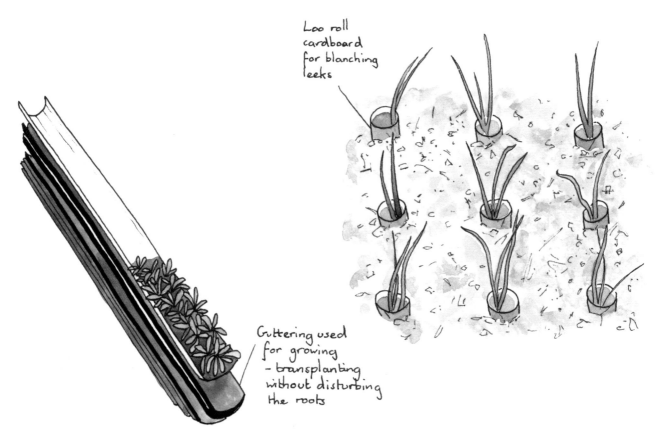

Loo roll cardboard for blanching leeks

Guttering used for growing – transplanting without disturbing the roots

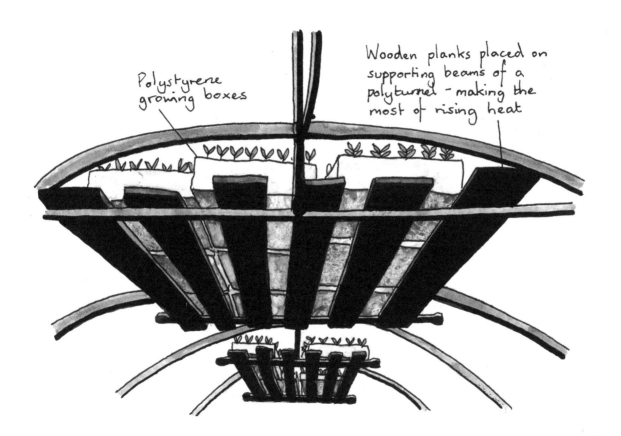

Polystyrene growing boxes

Wooden planks placed on supporting beams of a polytunnel - making the most of rising heat

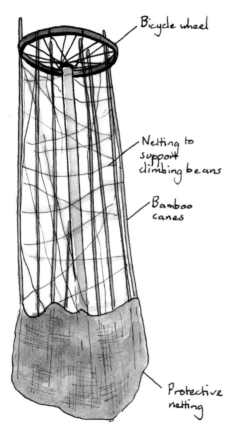

Bicycle wheel

Netting to support climbing beans

Bamboo canes

Protective netting

Shower door adapted to make a cold frame

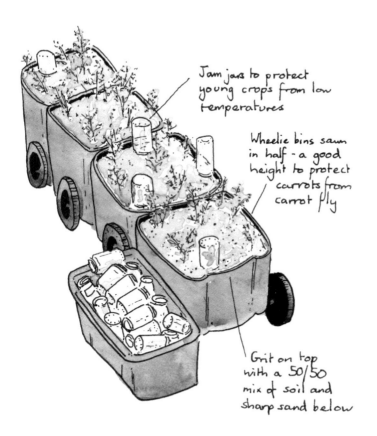

Jam jars to protect young crops from low temperatures

Wheelie bins sawn in half - a good height to protect carrots from carrot fly

Grit on top with a 50/50 mix of soil and sharp sand below

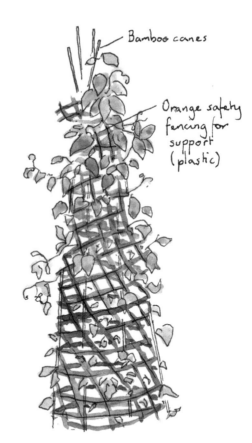

Bamboo canes

Orange safety fencing for support (plastic)

Weed Control

It isn't always possible to keep on top of the 'weed problem'. We're sometimes too busy with other things, or have perhaps taken on a neglected site, where the number of weeds is a daunting prospect. Temporarily covering areas of cleared soil with weed-control fabric is a way of slowing down regrowth, giving you time to tackle the rest of the plot.

- Household carpet can be used to suppress weeds on a patch of land. Make sure you pull it up after a couple of months though, otherwise the roots and carpet will become one!

- When planting out leeks, put newspapers down as a temporary weed suppressant and mulch. Plant out the seedlings into wide holes made in the newspaper. This means you don't have to hoe, risking filling up the leek holes with soil.

Using chemical-free cardboard to suppress weeds in the courgette patch

Protection

Aside from netting over the entire plot, there are less drastic steps you can take to protect crops from the likes of pigeons and cabbage white butterfly.

- Scaffolding netting is great for protecting larger crops such as brassicas. Drape over and attach to a curved frame, such as plastic piping or cut-open hula hoops.

- Build a fruit cage to cover the entire fruit patch.

- Cover young pea seedlings with small, spiky branches and twigs to deter pigeons.

- Some growers have actually been known to protect their crops from birds by netting over the entire plot!

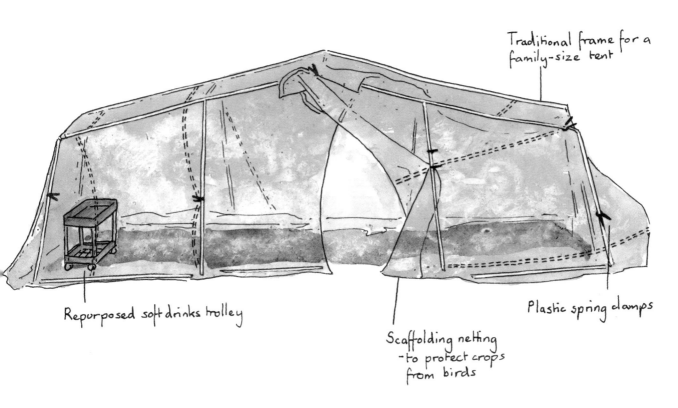

Traditional frame for a family-size tent

Repurposed soft drinks trolley

Scaffolding netting
- to protect crops
from birds

Plastic spring clamps

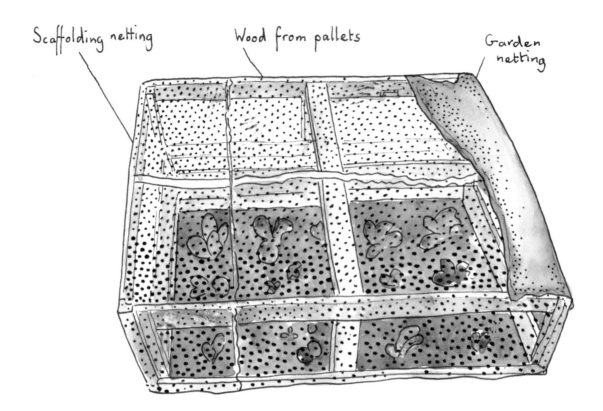

Scaffolding netting

Wood from pallets

Garden netting

Fine-mesh garden netting and canes - protects crops from carrot fly

Tin bath

Rogues Gallery

You rarely see a traditional scarecrow on an allotment – made out of stuffed sacks of hay or straw. Their clothing is usually 'pre-loved', but more often than not, their frames are instead cobbled together out of spare scrap wood, sticks and metal frames. Surreal figures abound, each protecting the plot from birds – and sometimes scaring off humans too!

- Keep hold of Halloween costumes and masks.

- Lucky enough to get hold of a shop dummy? Use that.

- Make a scarecrow in someone's image. They'll never figure it out. Or will they?

- Coconut shells make for good shrunken heads.

Fake plastic cabbages

Wilbur from *Charlotte's Web* made out of papier mâché

Wooden sculpture - eyes to guard the plot from thieves

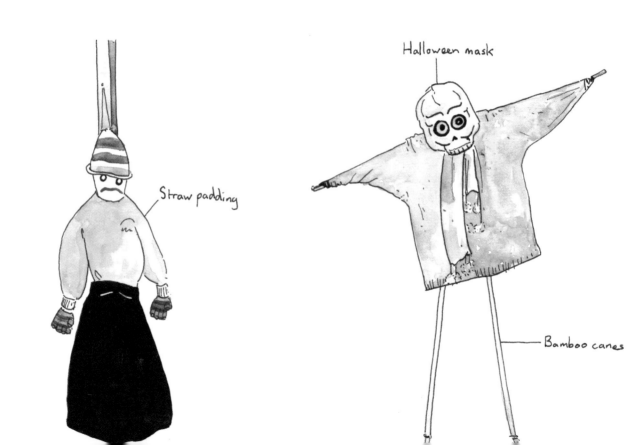

Straw padding

Halloween mask

Bamboo canes

Carousel ball
wind spinner
- spinning head

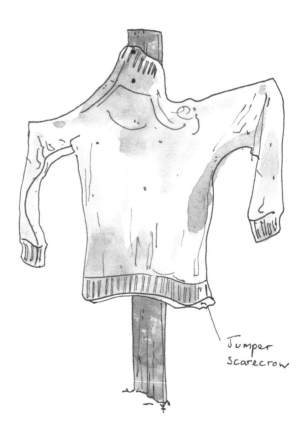

Jumper
Scarecrow

Storage

Storing both tools and salvaged materials can take up a lot of space. Sheds can easily lose their charm when crammed full with spare wood, metal and plastic. Being tidy helps you to keep on track with your sowing and planting. Try to keep stockpiling to a minimum by sharing materials with other growers when they need them. The favour will be returned at a later date.

- Keep bamboo canes together in one place by storing them in wide plastic pipes.

- Look out for old office storage equipment to kit your shed out with – filing cabinets, drawer units, etc.

- Build a wood store/shelter at the side of your shed.

- Try and give structures a dual purpose so they earn their keep. For example, a tool chest that is also a bench, or netting for climbing plants that also acts as a screen to hide salvaged materials.

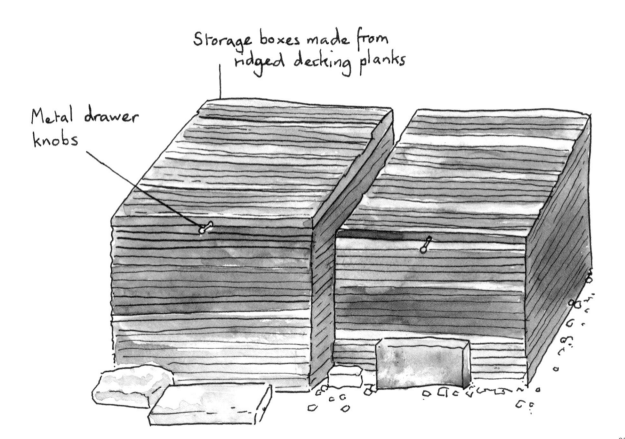

Storage boxes made from ridged decking planks

Metal drawer knobs

Half a pallet for
half-size tools

Fixed to wall

Old-fashioned
rake head
fixed to
interior shed
wall

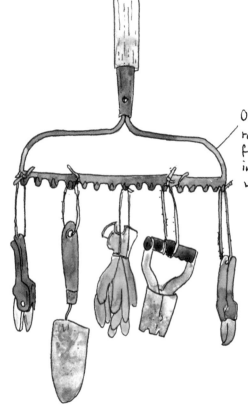

Old floppy disk storage box used to store seed packets

MAR-JULY

VEGETABLE EXPLORER

Harnessing the Sun

Allotment gardeners collect water, make compost, and some even have small windmills to convert wind into energy. So it makes sense to transfer energy from the sun too. Other than for suntans, some savvy growers have taken the harnessing of the sun's rays to the next level.

- Small solar power kits are affordable. They are often used to power lights, radios or charge batteries in allotment huts.

- Set up a solar powered irrigation system – collect rainwater from the roof, and have it pumped into the greenhouse by the power of the sun.

- Use mirrors to reflect available light into dark areas of the shed/greenhouse.

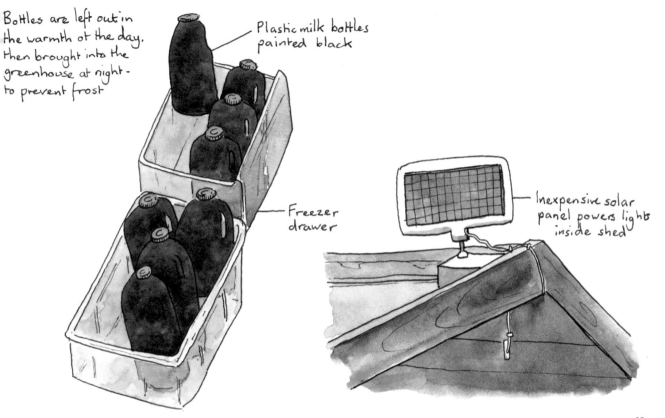

Bottles are left out in the warmth of the day, then brought into the greenhouse at night - to prevent frost

Plastic milk bottles painted black

Freezer drawer

Inexpensive solar panel powers lights inside shed

89

A shared indoor space is needed for committee meetings, open days, talks, shared meals, and the storage of shared tools and resources. They are mostly portacabins, as these need little repair for years to come, and can be locked up securely. Other sites have interesting repurposed structures that have been sourced locally, dismantled and then rebuilt on-site (scout huts, holiday chalets, free-standing garages).

- Research into available grants and funding opportunities for the design and installation of a purpose-built structure.

- Invite the local community to help paint a colourful allotment-themed mural on the side of the hut/portacabin.

- Some sites have a 'Trading Hut' where seeds and other gardening supplies can be bought at a discount price.

- Look out for 'his 'n' hers' portaloos.

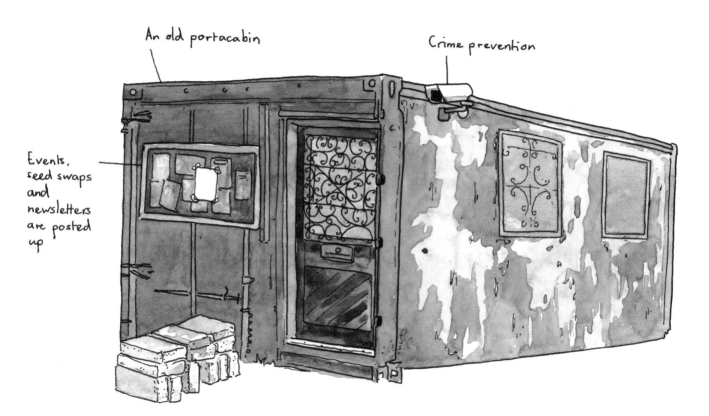

An old portacabin

Crime prevention

Events, seed swaps and newsletters are posted up

An old air station hut - dismantled and transported to the allotment site back in the 1950s

Trading hut is an old railway carriage

En Suite Bathrooms

Salvaged baths, sinks, toilets and bidets bring an instant hit of eccentricity to the plot. The old favourite 'there is a leak/leek in my bath' comes to mind. They are perfect as planters, and (with the added protection of a fine-mesh netting) are particularly good to grow carrots in – their height deters the low flying-female carrot flies.

- Tilt baths at a slight angle and line the bottom with rubble/stones to promote free-draining soil.

- Old bathroom cabinets are perfect for storing hand tools inside the shed – trowels and forks, etc.

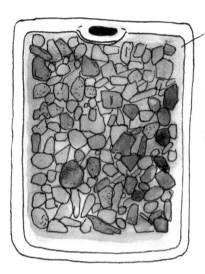

An old porcelain sink filled with broken tiles and stones - drainage, in preparation for planting up a mini herb garden

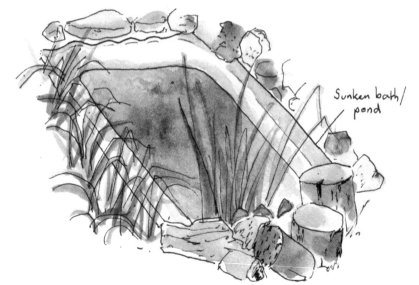

Sunken bath/ pond

Ornamental Flourishes

Everything needn't be purely functional...

- Start a collection of objects (bottle tops, tin cans, plastic bottles, wine bottles, etc.), and build something on a large scale – a colourful mosaic, a vertical growing space, or an unusual cold frame or wall.

- Wind chimes and mobiles have a dual purpose. They are pretty and the noise frightens the birds away so they don't eat your crops.

- Turn a wall into a mural, a plastic compost bin into a Dalek, fencing into piano keys or giant colouring pencils...

- Old technology becomes folk art – a decommissioned public telephone booth attached to the shed could be a 'talking point'.

- Make a mobile out of old CDs – the flashing of the light in the breeze will scare the birds away.

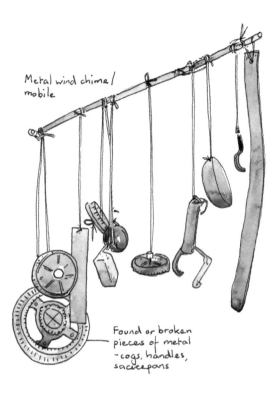

Metal wind chime / mobile

Found or broken pieces of metal – cogs, handles, saucepans

Shed mascot made from sweet jar lids and garden string

Bottle windmill - made from a plastic pop bottle

Coat hanger

Chopped up bottle tops rattle - scaring away pigeons

Bamboo cane

Chrome hubcaps
- scare away pigeons
- earrings for trees

Plot snake made from flexible orange piping

Useful Information

Get in touch with your local association to find allotment sites near you and for waiting list information, or visit: www.gov.uk/apply-allotment.

There are various regional and national associations you can join, either as an individual or as an allotment committee. These groups campaign on behalf of allotment users and offer advice and support to both new and established growers.

The National Allotment Society – www.nsalg.org.uk
Scottish Allotments and Gardens Society – www.sags.org.uk

The websites above offer lots of useful information and links to other community initiatives. However, for shed/structure building guidelines, you should contact your individual allotment sites directly, as each will be different.

For further advice on how to get the best out of your allotment, you can also visit: www.rhs.org.uk/advice/grow-your-own/allotments

With Thanks

A special mention to Judy and Rona for
their continued support and enthusiasm.

A warm thank you to Robin, Linda,
Harry, Dennis, Don and Annette.
Thanks for your generosity!

About the Author

'Allotments are curious, surrealist landscapes just waiting to be explored – an illustrator's dream.'

Emily Chappell is a Manchester-born illustrator and a graduate in Visual Communication from the Glasgow School of Art. Emily takes on a diverse range of commissions: her artwork is typically hand-drawn and acts as subtle social commentary.

Emily has been a plotholder at an urban allotment in Glasgow for over eight years and in this time has developed strong ties with the Glasgow Allotments Forum (GAF) and the Scottish Allotments and Gardens Society (SAGS). She has worked on many projects related to allotments, community gardens, growing and cooking – all of which influenced the making of this book. Emily strongly believes in a need for creative spaces – such as allotments – as places that encourage spontaneity, exploration, learning, sharing, restful activity and camaraderie.

Follow Emily on:
emilychappell.com
Instagram: @allotmenthuts
Twitter: @e_chappell